W9-CIA-991

HIP-HOP
Hitmakers

THE STORY OF
DEATH ROW
RECORDS

Trey White

MC Mason Crest
Philadelphia

HIP-HOP
hitmakers

Mason Crest
370 Reed Road
Broomall, PA 19008
www.masoncrest.com

Printed and bound in the United States of America.

CPSIA Compliance Information: Batch #HHH040112-4.
For further information, contact Mason Crest at 1-866-MCP-Book

First printing
1 3 5 7 9 8 6 4 2

Library of Congress Cataloging-in-Publication Data

White, Trey.
 The story of Death Row Records / Trey White.
    p. cm. — (Hip-hop hitmakers)
 Includes bibliographical references and index.
 ISBN 978-1-4222-2113-6 (hc)
 ISBN 978-1-4222-2126-6 (pb)
 ISBN 978-1-4222-9465-9 (ebook)
 1. Death Row Records—History. 2. Record labels. I. Title.
 ML3792.D43W55 2012
 338.7'61782421649—dc23
                              2011035323

Photo credits: Associated Press: 54; Getty Images: 12, 33, 51, 52; Time & Life Pictures/Getty Images: 27, 48; Mike Segar / Reuters / Landov: 50; PR Newswire: 24; used under license from Shutterstock, Inc.: 7, 19, 34 (top); Carroteater / Shutterstock.com: 20; Songquan Deng / Shutterstock.com: 47; Helga Esteb / Shutterstock.com: 16; Featureflash / Shutterstock.com: 10; Steven Pepple / Shutterstock.com: 34 (bottom); Lev Radin / Shutterstock.com: 32; Adam J. Sablich / Shutterstock.com: 23; Tristan Scholze / Shutterstock.com: 15; Joe Seer / Shutterstock.com: 45; WireImage: cover, 4, 36, 41, 53.

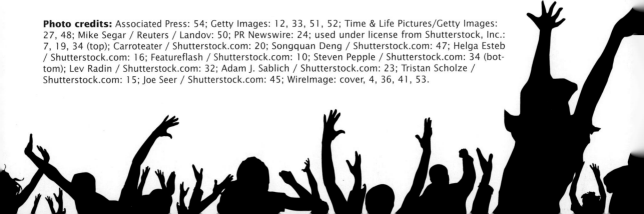

Contents

Marion "Suge" Knight founded a music label that released some of the best-selling albums in hip-hop history.

1

Setting the Stage

I t reads like a movie script: A boy from a tough, gang-infested neighborhood stays out of trouble, does well in school, and grows up to be a college football star. After his dreams of a pro football career stall, he seems aimless. He has a serious brush with the law and appears headed for prison. Instead, he receives *probation.*

With this new lease on life, he finds work as a bodyguard for a famous R&B singer. He takes full advantage of the opportunity. He learns all he can about the music industry. Soon he is promoting local concerts. Next he starts his own music publishing company and his own management company. After that, still just 25 years old, he launches a record label.

For a few brief, shining years that label and its chief executive officer (CEO) stand atop the hip-hop world. They take hard-core gangsta rap into the mainstream, selling millions of records. And the money rolls in. There are mansions, a yacht, a fleet of luxury cars, even a Las Vegas nightclub.

But all the while, disturbing rumors of gang influence swirl around the record label and its CEO. There are also regular incidents of violence. It seems that the gangster lifestyle depicted—and, critics would say, *glamorized*—in the label's most popular recordings has spilled over into the business.

In the end, the hip-hop empire is brought down by all the mayhem. One of the label's biggest stars is gunned down. At least eight other associates of the label's CEO will also be murdered. He is sent to prison. His top artists move on. Though his record label has generated up to $750 million in revenue in 15 years, the CEO is broke. He files for bankruptcy. Two years later, his label is sold at auction.

It sounds like fiction—the plot, perhaps, of some Hollywood movie. But it's not. It's the true story of Death Row Records and its cofounder and CEO, Suge Knight.

"SUGAR BEAR"

Suge Knight was born Marion Hugh Knight Jr. in Los Angeles, California, on April 19, 1965. Suge, pronounced like the first syllable of "sugar," is a shortening of the future hip-hop *mogul*'s childhood nickname. According to his mother, Maxine, her son's consistently sweet demeanor prompted the family to call him Sugar Bear.

Sugar Bear was the only boy and the youngest of the three children of Maxine Knight and her husband, Marion Knight Sr. The family lived in a small two-bedroom house in Compton, a city of nearly 100,000 residents located southeast of downtown Los Angeles.

Marion Knight Sr. made his living as a truck driver. But he had two

Suge Knight made Los Angeles the capital of his gangsta rap empire.

abiding passions: football and music. In his youth, he had been both an excellent football player and a singer in a local R&B group. He passed on his love of football and music to his son.

STAYING OFF THE MEAN STREETS

By his teen years, Suge (he had by this time shortened the cuddly nickname of his childhood) was showing a lot of ability on the football field. And he was very, very big. At Lynwood High School, where he played on the varsity football squad, he stood 6'3" tall and tipped the scales at more than 270 pounds. But he didn't fit the mold of the loutish jock. He was serious about his studies, and he brought home good grades.

Compton during this time was experiencing a surge in violence. Much of it was due to fighting between the Crips and the Bloods, two powerful African-American gangs that had spread south from Los Angeles. Many black youths from Compton joined one or the other of the rival gangs. In the process, some lost their lives to the gang warfare. Many others were arrested and sent to prison for their involvement in the criminal activities associated with the gangs, especially the selling of illegal drugs. A sense of fear, anger, and hopelessness hung over many Compton neighborhoods like a pall.

Much has been made of Suge Knight's association with a Compton-based set, or subgroup, of the Bloods called the Mob Piru.

THE CRIPS AND BLOODS

The Crips and the Bloods—who are sworn enemies—are two of the most feared African-American street gangs in the United States. Both gangs are involved in all sorts of crime, from the selling of illegal drugs to armed robbery to murder. Neither gang, however, is a unified organization with a centralized leadership structure. Rather, the Crips and the Bloods are both "umbrella" gangs. Under their respective "brand names" are a host of loosely linked local gangs, or sets.

The Crips were started in Los Angeles around 1969. Initially, the members were all pretty young. But the Crips soon became very powerful. They began to force out other street gangs and take control of many poor black sections of L.A. Their influence also began to expand outside of the city.

Around 1972, a handful of non-Crip gangs—including the Piru Street Boys of Compton—formed an alliance to counter the growing power of the Crips. They called themselves the Bloods.

Today Crips and Bloods sets exist in many American cities. The gangs even have a presence in some foreign countries.

It's unclear when that association began. What does seem clear is that, whether or not he joined the Mob Piru Bloods as a teenager, Suge wasn't a hard-core member. He didn't get into any trouble with the law. He was focused on getting into college and pursuing a career in football.

FOOTBALL DREAMS

Suge entered El Camino College, located in Los Angeles County, in 1983. He played well enough on the junior college's football team to attract the attention of recruiters from the University of Nevada, Las Vegas (UNLV). In 1985, after graduating from El Camino with an *associate's degree*, he entered UNLV on a full football scholarship.

Suge, now 6'4" tall and weighing more than 300 pounds, played defensive end for UNLV. After his first season, the young man from Compton was voted the team's rookie of the year. He followed that up with another standout season the following year. "He was Super Bowl material," former UNLV head football coach Harvey Hyde would later recall, "the kind of guy you loved having on your side."

Despite having made the dean's list at UNLV, Suge dropped out before getting his degree. He still dreamed of a career in the National Football League. That never came to pass. But he did, briefly, get a chance to play in the NFL. Early in the 1987 season, the regular players went on strike. Rather than canceling the season, team owners decided to hire replacement players. Suge played two games for the Los Angeles Rams' replacement

FAST FACT

During the 1987 strike by the players union, NFL teams fielded replacement squads for three weeks of competition. The replacement players each received $4,000 per game. Like Suge Knight, almost all were cut immediately after the strike ended.

squad. When the strike was settled, he was cut. A later tryout with the Rams failed to pan out.

A NEW PATH

In 1987, Suge Knight had the first of what would be many serious brushes with the law. He got into a fight during which, apparently, his foe brandished a gun. Suge took the gun away from the other man and shot him with it. Fortunately, the wound wasn't serious. Suge fled the scene in the man's car.

He was soon arrested and charged with attempted murder, auto theft, and carrying a concealed weapon. If convicted on all the charges, Suge could have received a long prison sentence. But he had no prior criminal record, and his lawyer and the prosecutor worked out a deal. Suge pleaded *no contest* to the weapons charge, and he was given probation.

After his legal troubles were resolved, Suge became a bodyguard for Bobby Brown. An R&B singer, Brown had gotten his start with the boy band New Edition. His first solo album, 1986's *King of Stage*, spawned the single "Girlfriend," which reached #1 on the Billboard R&B charts. Brown's next album, *Don't Be Cruel*

Suge Knight started working in the music industry as a bodyguard for R&B singer Bobby Brown.

(1988), was a blockbuster. It sold 8 million copies and included five songs that charted in the top 10 on Billboard's Hot 100 singles list.

While working for Brown, Suge Knight began considering the possibility of making a career for himself in the music industry. He started promoting concerts. Then, in 1989, he founded a music publishing company. For this business, Suge hired a small stable of obscure songwriters to compose songs.

The following year, he branched out, founding a company to manage the careers of musical artists. Among the first people he represented were DJ Quik, an MC from Compton, and The D.O.C., a rapper and songwriter from Dallas, Texas. Suge's unusual work on behalf of another artist from Dallas would go a long way toward establishing his gangster reputation in the music industry.

CHOCOLATE VS. VANILLA

In 1990, SBK Records released an album titled *To the Extreme*. It was the major-label **debut** of Vanilla Ice, a white rapper from Dallas whose real name is Robert Van Winkle. *To the Extreme* was a huge success. It rocketed to #1 on the Billboard 200 albums chart and eventually sold more than 11 million copies worldwide.

One of the album's tracks, "Ice Ice Baby," became the first hip-hop song ever to reach #1 on the Billboard Hot 100 singles chart. That song would become the center of a huge controversy.

Mario "Chocolate" Johnson, a rapper and songwriter originally from Dallas, claimed he had written and produced "Ice Ice Baby." But he hadn't received any credit for, or *royalties* from, the song. Johnson, who had since moved to Los Angeles, turned to Suge Knight to correct the situation.

Vanilla Ice (center) performs his hit "Ice Ice Baby" during a 1990 concert. The rapper was eventually persuaded to sign over rights to the song to Suge Knight's client, Mario Johnson.

Such matters are usually settled with lawsuits. But Suge had different ideas. Accompanied by two other huge men, he introduced himself to Vanilla Ice at a Hollywood restaurant. Suge and his companions plopped down at the table where the rapper was eating. According to Randall Sullivan, author of the book *LAbyrinth*, which details some of the violence associated with Death Row Records, the three men stared silently at Vanilla Ice for several minutes before Suge explained what he wanted. In the weeks that followed, Vanilla Ice received several other menacing visits.

The situation finally came to a head at Hollywood's Bel Age Hotel. Suge, Mario Johnson, and another man barged into Vanilla Ice's 15th-floor suite there. Suge took Ice out onto the balcony. Reports of what happened next vary. At one time, Ice claimed that Suge hoisted him up by the ankles and dangled him over the railing. Later he insisted this never happened. By he did say that Suge threatened to throw him off the balcony if he didn't sign over songwriting rights to "Ice Ice Baby."

=== **FAST FACT** ===

The single "Ice Ice Baby" brought Vanilla Ice problems besides his run-in with Suge Knight. The song sampled the bass line from "Under Pressure," a 1981 hit by David Bowie and Queen. But Vanilla Ice hadn't received permission from or credited them. Eventually, Vanilla Ice paid Bowie and Queen an undisclosed amount of money to avoid a lawsuit.

Whatever occurred at the Bel Age Hotel that day, Vanilla Ice got the message. He did as Suge Knight demanded. And Suge made a tidy sum of money from his share of Johnson's royalties from "Ice Ice Baby."

Suge had set the stage for an even bigger push into the hip-hop world. His next move would rock the industry to its foundations.

2

the birth of death Row

The D.O.C., whose career Suge Knight managed, had done some songwriting work for a hip-hop group from Compton called N.W.A. The D.O.C. introduced Suge to one of N.W.A.'s members, Dr. Dre.

Dre, whose real name is Andre Young, wasn't happy with his current situation. He'd done most of the production work for N.W.A.'s 1988 album *Straight Outta Compton*. The hard-core gangsta rap album had been an underground sensation. With virtually no advance publicity and no airplay, it had sold more than 2 million copies on the Ruthless Records label. Dre also was the main producer for other Ruthless Records artists. Yet he wasn't receiving much money. He believed that the president of Ruthless Records, Eric "Eazy-E"

Wright—who also happened to be a member of N.W.A.—and Ruthless cofounder Jerry Heller (N.W.A.'s manager) were treating him unfairly.

Dre wasn't alone in his grievances. In 1990, N.W.A. member Ice Cube left the group after a bitter contract dispute.

Around the same time, Dr. Dre sought the help of Suge Knight. "Dre approached me and asked me if I would go over his contracts," Suge recalled.

> At the time, [Ruthless Records] wouldn't even give him a copy of his own agreement, but I got a hold of one on my own. We found out that Cube was right. Ruthless was taking Dre for a ride. And not just Dre, every other artist on the roster too. Man, we opened up a real can of worms.

With Dr. Dre's blessing, Suge set about convincing Ruthless to release Dre and two other artists from their contracts. According to Eazy-E, the "negotiations" were brief. Suge and two other men showed up at a recording studio where Eazy-E was working. They

Rapper Ice Cube left the groundbreaking group N.W.A. after a dispute with Ruthless Records founder Eazy-E. His departure encouraged Dr. Dre to break away from the label as well.

In 1991, talented music producer Andre "Dr. Dre" Young co-founded Death Row Records with Suge Knight.

were wielding baseball bats and metal pipes. Jerry Heller told a similar story about being intimidated into agreeing to release Dr. Dre. Heller filed a lawsuit. Suge Knight, however, denied the allegations, and the lawsuit was later dismissed.

MAKING HIP-HOP HISTORY

In 1991, after the successful resolution of the contract disputes with Ruthless, Suge Knight launched his own record label with Dr. Dre. Suge would handle the business side of the operation while Dre focused on creative matters.

Suge later explained to a reporter for *Vibe* magazine about how they had come up with a name for their label. "We called it Death Row," he said, "'cause most everybody had been involved with the law."

This was hardly an exaggeration. Suge himself had been arrested again, in 1990. This time the charge was *battery*. The case was eventually dismissed. Dre, too, had recently been arrested for assaulting a female TV host in a nightclub. Other Death Row artists had criminal records for a range of violent offenses. Troubles with the law extended even to much of Death Row's support staff: many of the company's security guards and office employees were members of the Mob Piru Bloods. This would figure in much of the later violence linked to Death Row.

From the standpoint of fan acceptance, the association of Death Row Records with crime wasn't a problem. If anything, it was a plus. Death Row's signature would be hard-core gangsta rap. Its artists would rap about growing up poor and black, about drugs and violence and the mean streets of America's ghettos, about the brutality and corruption of police. Criminal records added to the artists' credibility, demonstrating that they lived in the tough worlds about which they rapped.

Early on, however, Suge Knight's growing reputation as a thug, his associates' involvement in crime, and the nature of gangsta rap music—which contained language and themes many people found offensive— seem to have frightened away potential distributors for Death Row's releases. None of the major players in the music industry wanted to touch Death Row. It took Suge a year before he finally sealed a deal with Interscope, a small, independent label.

=== FAST FACT ===

Motown's roster of superstar artists included Smokey Robinson & the Miracles, Diana Ross & the Supremes, the Temptations, Stevie Wonder, and the Jackson 5.

From the outset, Suge Knight had big plans for Death Row. He famously declared that he wanted to make his label "the Motown of the '90s." Like that Detroit-based, black-owned record label, he was aiming to create a distinctive musical style that had major *crossover* appeal. At first glance, however, his task would be much more difficult than that of Berry Gordy, Motown's founder. Between 1961 and 1971, Gordy and his producers had scored more than 100 top 10 hits by starting with soul music and adding radio-friendly, pop elements. Death Row would be starting with gangsta rap. It was unclear whether that *genre* would ever appeal to a broad-based—or, to put it in racial terms, white—audience.

DRE SCORES BIG

In late 1992, with Interscope as the distributor, Death Row released its first album: Dr. Dre's *The Chronic*. The impact was immediate and enormous.

Commercially, *The Chronic* was a huge success. In less than a year, the album was certified triple-platinum (meaning 3 million copies had been sold) by the Recording Industry Association of America (RIAA). Eventually more than 8 million copies would be sold worldwide. Three of the album's singles broke onto the Billboard Hot 100 pop charts. They included "Nuthin' but a 'G' Thang," which peaked at #2. Suge Knight's notion that gangsta rap could gain crossover appeal didn't seem so far-fetched now.

Artistically, *The Chronic* was a *tour de force*. Many critics quickly recognized it as a hip-hop masterpiece, and time hasn't diminished the album's reputation. In 2003, when *Rolling Stone* published a list of the 500 greatest albums of all time—in any genre—*The Chronic* ranked

137. The album appeared on *Time*'s 2006 list of the top 100 albums ever (the selections weren't otherwise ranked). *Spin* magazine's 2010 list of the 125 best albums from the previous 25 years had *The Chronic* at number 82.

The 16 tracks on Dre's solo debut covered familiar themes of gangsta rap, such as drugs, crime, and violence. One track celebrated the riots that tore through South Central Los Angeles and claimed the lives of 53 people in late April and early May 1992, after police officers on trial for the beating of black motorist Rodney King were found not guilty. Other typical characteristics of gangsta rap were in

CERTIFYING SALES: THE RIAA

The Recording Industry Association of America (RIAA) is a trade organization whose membership consists of American record labels. The RIAA's mission is to help defend the free-speech rights of musical artists and labels, as well as to prevent the songs or albums of its members from being pirated.

The RIAA also certifies how many copies of a single or album have been sold. The organization has awards to mark milestones in sales. A Gold award signifies the sale of 500,000 copies. Platinum denotes a million copies sold. The Multi-Platinum award is given after a single or album crosses the 2 million sales threshold. The RIAA's

Diamond award is reserved for singles or albums that sell 10 million copies.

For The Chronic, *Dre drew on the sound of 1970s funk music. The innovative musician George Clinton was a strong influence on Dre's new hip-hop sound, which came to be known as G-funk.*

evidence throughout *The Chronic,* including the use of very *explicit* language, an attitude of contempt for women, and disses directed at other rappers (in this case Eazy-E and Ruthless Records).

Where *The Chronic* was truly groundbreaking was in its production. Dre crafted a distinctive style called G-funk. He blended influences from jazz, soul, and especially funk, *sampling* from sources such as funk pioneer George Clinton and the 1970s groups Parliament and Funkadelic but deliberately slowing down the beat. Layers of synthesizers, live instrumental performances, and background vocals gave Dre's G-funk a musical intricacy not previously heard in rap. The sound, in the words of a *Rolling Stone* reviewer, was "as raw and complex and real as life." G-funk would set the course for gangsta rap for several years to come. It would, in fact, influence all hip-hop music.

The success of *The Chronic* also signaled the beginning of a shift in the hip-hop world's center of gravity. For years, the East Coast had been producing the bulk of rap's most commercially successful and artistically cutting-edge music. Increasingly, the West Coast would dominate. And there would be no bigger power in the West than Los Angeles–based Death Row Records.

A STABLE OF TALENT

Dr. Dre had tapped the talents of a number of young guest performers for *The Chronic*. They included Daz Dillinger and Kurupt, who formed the rap duo Tha Dogg Pound; The Lady of Rage; and Nate Dogg. In the years that followed, all would chart their own successes with Death Row.

But none of the guest performers on *The Chronic* created as much excitement as—or would achieve more commercial success than—Snoop Doggy Dogg. Dre had signed Snoop to Death Row Records, and the 21-year-old rapper performed on 12 of *The Chronic*'s 16 tracks. Snoop shone. His talent was especially evident on "Nuthin' but a 'G' Thang," which Snoop wrote. Hip-hop fans and critics alike were taken by his clever lyrics and seemingly effortless rap flow.

Fans clamored for a solo album from Snoop. They wouldn't have to wait long.

3

making hits

s the summer of 1993 came to a close, Snoop Doggy Dogg was among the most famous rappers in the country. Snoop—whose real name is Cordazar Calvin Broadus— had yet to release an album of his own. But he'd made a big splash on Dr. Dre's *The Chronic*. The top music magazines had featured Snoop on their covers, and hip-hop fans eagerly awaited a solo offering from the smooth-rapping MC.

Snoop had also gotten a lot of publicity for the wrong reasons. On August 25, 1993, he'd been involved in a fatal shooting in the Woodbine Park section of Los Angeles. The details remain murky, but the shooting apparently stemmed from a gang dispute. Earlier in the day, members of Snoop's crew—the rapper himself wasn't present—

22

were standing near a building. A car filled with gangbangers, including 22-year-old Philip Waldemariam, drove up. They believed Snoop's crew to be members of a rival gang, which may or may not have been the case—Snoop, at least, had been in the Crips. In any event, insults were exchanged before the men in the car drove off. Later, Snoop and his crew encountered the gangbangers at a park. The dispute flared up again. When Waldemariam approached Snoop's Jeep, the rapper's bodyguard, McKinley Lee, opened fire. He would claim that Waldemariam had been reaching for a gun. Snoop, who was driving the Jeep, sped off. On September 2, a few hours after appearing at the MTV Music Video Awards in Los Angeles, Snoop was arrested. He, Lee, and another passenger in the Jeep, Sean Smith, were charged with murder.

Snoop Doggy Dogg's relaxed style of rapping made him one of hip-hop's biggest stars during the 1990s.

A DOGG'S WORLD

In the world of gangsta rap, however, a murder charge was no obstacle to success. In November 1993, when Death Row Records released Snoop Doggy Dogg's debut solo album, *Doggystyle*, hip-hop fans rushed to buy it. *Doggystyle* became the first rap album ever to enter the Billboard 200 pop charts at #1. Within two months, it had sold an astounding 3 million copies. It would eventually be certified 4X platinum (meaning it sold 4 million copies) by the RIAA.

Dre with his protégé Snoop Doggy Dogg. Doggystyle, *produced by Dre, was another huge success for Death Row.*

The commercial success of *Doggystyle* was matched by the critical acclaim. Many music writers hailed the album as an instant classic of hip-hop.

Dr. Dre, who had taken Snoop Doggy Dogg under his wing after signing the young rapper to Death Row, served as the producer of *Doggystyle*. The album bore the hallmarks of Dre's G-funk sound, and in the opinion of some music critics, Dre had topped his groundbreaking work from *The Chronic*. "Dre's production takes hip-hop to another level," wrote Jonathan Gold, music critic for the *Los Angeles Times*, "organic yet relentless, the air alive with sleigh bells, sighs, countermelodies, wisps of Temptations-style backing vocals and low-mixed call-and-response that seems to float in from the ether."

Most writers and hip-hop fans believed that Snoop's rapping was an ideal complement to Dre's production wizardry. "His relaxed vocal style is a perfect match for Dr. Dre's bass-heavy producing," wrote *Time* magazine's Christopher John Farley. "The songs on this album are built around '70s-style funk grooves; Snoop's voice is lithe enough to snake its way around the big beats. Tracks like 'Aint No Fun (If the Homies Cant Have None)' are perfectly crafted to come booming out of Jeeps and college dorms."

Snoop's rhymes weren't necessarily as clever as those of other rappers. Yet his flow was unsurpassed. "No rapper," declared Jonathan Gold of the *Los Angeles Times*, "has ever occupied a beat the way Snoop does, sliding around corners, lounging on the syncopations, slipping into the cracks and crevices of the grooves."

=**FAST FACT**=

Doggystyle broke the music industry record for first-week album sales. Nearly 803,000 copies were sold in the period November 23–30, 1993.

As far as content was concerned, *Doggystyle* fell squarely into the category of hard-core gangsta rap. Snoop made frequent references to guns and gangs and blowing away rivals. He held forth about the pleasures of getting high. He rapped about using women. The language was very explicit.

Yet one track, "Murder Was the Case," offered a glimpse at a more thoughtful, spiritual Snoop—one who saw the emptiness of the gangster life. In the track, Snoop imagines himself as the victim of a gang shooting. He is on the brink of death and comes face-to-face with God:

> I think it's too late for prayin, hold up
> A voice spoke to me and it slowly started sayin
> "Bring your lifestyle to me I'll make it better"
> How long will I live?
> "Eternal life and forever"
> And will I be, the G that I was?
> "I'll make your life better than you can imagine
>   or even dreamed of
> So relax your soul, let me take control
> Close your eyes my son"
> My eyes are closed

Snoop insisted that the true message of *Doggystyle* was one of peace and love. He wasn't glamorizing gang violence, drug abuse, or other destructive behavior, he said. He actually wanted to steer African-American youth away from that lifestyle, which he'd become entangled in growing up in a blighted area of Long Beach. "I feel like it's my job to play the backup role for parents who can't get it across to their kids," Snoop told a writer for the *New York Times*. "For little kids growing up in the ghettos, it's easy to get into the wrong types of things, especially gangbanging and selling drugs. I've seen what that was like, and I don't glorify it, but I don't preach."

OBJECTIONS

Not everyone took Snoop at his word. Many people heard *Doggystyle*—in addition to *The Chronic* and other gangsta rap offerings—as nothing *but* a glorification of violence, the humiliation of women, and other bad behavior. One such person was the African-American activist C. Delores Tucker. Shortly after the release of *Doggystyle*, Tucker launched a campaign against gangsta rap. As that genre's most important label, Death Row received much of the focus of Tucker's crusade.

Gangsta rap critic C. Delores Tucker (1927–2005) was a longtime civil rights activist and political figure. In 1971, she was appointed Pennsylvania's secretary of state, becoming the first African American to serve in such a position anywhere in the United States.

Suge Knight met repeatedly with Tucker. Publicly, the two professed respect for each other. Yet the activist never succeeded in convincing the record mogul that gangsta rap was eroding the moral foundation of the African-American community by stoking deadly violence and encouraging the mistreatment of women. Tucker's campaign against gangsta rap would eventually have serious consequences for Death Row's business. Initially, however, her calls for people to *boycott* gangsta rap and record stores that sold it had little effect.

With the runaway success of *The Chronic* and *Doggystyle*, Death Row was rolling in money. And in 1994, the label scored another hit with the soundtrack to the motion picture *Above the Rim*. Released in

DOGG'S LIFE

Snoop Doggy Dogg—who would drop the "Doggy" from his stage name after leaving Death Row Records—was born on October 20, 1971, in Long Beach, California. His birth name was Cordozar Calvin Broadus.

Growing up, he got into a fair amount of trouble with the law, mostly for drug-related offenses. Snoop was a member of the Crips. After graduating from Long Beach Polytechnic High School, he spent time in and out of jail for several years.

The course of Snoop's life changed when he started making rap tapes with his best friend, Warren Griffin III. Griffin, better known as Warren G, is the stepbrother of Dr. Dre. Upon hearing the rap tapes, Dre instantly recognized Snoop's talent. He signed the young rapper to Death Row Records.

Since the release of his solo debut, *Doggystyle*, Snoop has been one of hip-hop's biggest stars. He has also acted on TV shows and in movies, including *Training Day* (2001) and *Starsky & Hutch* (2004).

March, the album sold more than 2 million copies. It reached #2 on the Billboard 200 pop charts.

The soundtrack featured performances by a number of Death Row artists. Two of the 18 tracks were laid down by Tha Dogg Pound (Daz Dillinger and Kurupt). The Lady of Rage and Snoop Doggy Dogg collaborated on "Afro Puffs." Warren G got help from Nate Dogg on "Regulate."

The track "Pour out a Little Liquor" was performed by an up-and-coming rapper originally from New York City: Tupac Shakur. In the movie *Above the Rim*, Tupac (also known as 2Pac) had played the role of a young thug named Biggie. In portraying the character, he was no doubt able to draw on his own experience. Tupac had been arrested multiple times, and he'd served a couple short stints in jail for assault. At the time of the movie's release, he was facing trial on serious charges that could land him in prison for a long time.

LEGAL MATTERS

Tupac hadn't yet signed with Death Row. But his troubles with the law mirrored the legal difficulties the label's major players were experiencing.

Snoop Doggy Dogg faced the most uncertain future. He was awaiting trial for the fatal shooting of Philip Waldemariam.

Dr. Dre was looking at jail time after his arrest for DUI (driving under the influence of alcohol) on January 10, 1994. When Los Angeles police apprehended him that night after a high-speed chase, Dre's blood alcohol level was twice the legal limit. The DUI violated the terms of Dre's probation for assaulting record producer Damon Thomas in 1992—one of at least three assaults on Dre's rap sheet.

A criminal case against Suge Knight—for assault with a deadly weapon—was also wending its way through the court system in early 1994. Two years earlier, the Death Row president had viciously beaten two young rappers—George and Lynwood Stanley—with a pistol. The Stanley brothers had angered him by using a studio telephone without his permission. Suge also faced charges of possession of an illegal firearm, stemming from an unrelated incident that occurred in early 1994.

Many critics condemned the thuggish attitude Death Row Records seemingly embraced. Even fans would be shocked by the violence that swirled around the label in the years to come.

hip-hop Superpower

n October 1994, Death Row released another soundtrack album, *Murder Was the Case*. Like the soundtrack for *Above the Rim*, it contained performances by many Death Row artists. They included Snoop Doggy Dogg; Dre, who reunited with former N.W.A. mate Ice Cube for one track; Tha Dogg Pound; Nate Dogg; and Danny Boy, a 17-year-old R&B singer from Chicago whom Suge Knight had discovered. Like the *Above the Rim* soundtrack, *Murder Was the Case* proved highly popular. It rocketed to #1 on the Billboard 200 albums chart, eventually selling more than 2 million copies.

What set Death Row's second soundtrack apart was the fact that it didn't accompany someone else's movie. Rather, it went with a film produced by Death Row. Directed by Dre and hip-hop artist Fab 5

Fab 5 Freddy, a hip-hop pioneer, co-directed the short 1994 film Murder Was the Case *for Death Row Records.*

Freddy (Fred Brathwaite), the 18-minute film *Murder Was the Case* was inspired by Snoop's earlier song of the same title. It depicted his killing and resurrection.

Suge Knight viewed *Murder Was the Case,* produced for about $750,000, as the first step in Death Row's entry into feature films. He also planned to launch a music magazine under the label's umbrella. Clearly, Suge's ambitions extended well beyond heading a gangsta rap record label—even if it was the biggest, most successful one in the field. He dreamed of establishing an entertainment empire.

OF PROFIT AND PRINCIPLE

There's no doubt that Suge enjoyed the wheeling and dealing of the business world, or that he constantly sought to prove his skills as a business executive. He admitted as much on numerous occasions. But by all accounts he also was driven by loyalty to his artists. "I try to do everything in my power to protect the people I love and to make sure everybody in the Death Row family prospers," he told a writer for

The huge success of Death Row's releases made Suge Knight extremely wealthy.

Spin magazine. He said his dream was "to make Dre and Snoop and every artist on this label a multimillionaire." And this, Suge suggested, was what really irked many people—particularly the white establishment—about Death Row. "I know there are still individuals in this society," he said, "who can't stand the thought of a young black person with a [ton] of money in the bank."

Gangsta rap's defenders insisted that the music simply reflected the crime, drug use, gang violence, and despair common in America's decaying inner cities.

C. Delores Tucker would insist that her issues with Death Row had nothing to do with money. She simply objected to the lyrics of gangsta rap music, which she called "pornographic filth." Some well-known African Americans publicly agreed with Tucker's claim that gangsta rap not only spread negative stereotypes of blacks but also contributed to crime, violence, and the mistreatment of women in the African-American community. Others, though, believed Tucker was missing the point. Gangsta rap, they said, depicted the horrible conditions that actually existed in inner-city ghettos. People who were truly concerned about the state of black America should work to change those conditions rather than trying to muzzle the rappers.

Time Warner, a huge media corporation, owned 50 percent of Interscope, Death Row's distributor. Tucker purchased 10 shares of Time Warner stock so that she could air her objections to gangsta rap at the company's 1995 shareholders' meeting. At that meeting, she asked Time Warner executives to recite the lyrics to some of the gangsta rap music Interscope had distributed. The executives declined, driving home Tucker's point that the lyrics were offensive. Still, Time Warner took no action. Company officials insisted that rappers had the right to free expression, just like every American. Tucker countered that Time Warner was "putting profit before principle."

Tucker refused to abandon her campaign, and she enlisted a famous and powerful ally: William Bennett. A self-proclaimed champion of traditional values and morality, Bennett—who is white—had served as the U.S. secretary of education and as head of the Office of National Drug Control Policy. During the summer of 1995, he and Tucker launched a national advertising campaign that targeted Time Warner's support for gangsta rap.

Bad Boy Entertainment founder Sean "Puffy" Combs (right) attends a 1995 awards show with his label's biggest star, Christoper "Notorious B.I.G." Wallace. The New York–based label would soon find itself involved in a feud with rappers from Death Row.

The pressure worked. In late September 1995, Time Warner announced its decision to sell its stake in Interscope. Death Row would have to get by without benefit of Time Warner's huge marketing resources.

THE EAST COAST–WEST COAST FEUD

Even before the split between Time Warner and Interscope was official, Suge Knight had embroiled Death Row Records in another controversy. This one would have deadly consequences.

It began at New York City's Paramount Theater on the night of August 3, 1995. The event was the second annual Source Hip-Hop Music Awards. In attendance were the biggest stars in the rap world, including many artists from two of the most powerful labels: Bad Boy Entertainment, headquartered in New York City, and L.A.-based Death Row.

Onstage to present one of the awards, Suge Knight told the assembled artists, "If you don't want the owner of your label on your album or in your video or on your tour, come sign with Death Row." Though he hadn't mentioned any names, everyone knew that Suge was referring to the founder of Bad Boy, Sean "Puff Daddy" Combs, who had a habit of sharing the spotlight with his artists. Likewise, everyone knew that Suge was both dissing Combs and issuing a business challenge. Many also interpreted the Death Row mogul's comments as an insult to Bad Boy's artists and East Coast rappers in general.

FAST FACT

Sean Combs has been known by various names since founding Bad Boy in 1990: Puffy, Puff Daddy, P. Diddy, and simply Diddy.

Witnesses have said that Combs was visibly shaken by Suge Knight's remarks. Later, when it came time for him to present an award—as fate would have it, to Death Row's Snoop Doggy Dogg— Puff Daddy hugged Snoop and spoke of the need for "unity" in the hip-hop world. But there would be no such unity.

On September 24, Suge Knight and Sean Combs, along with members of their respective *entourages*, were at a club in Atlanta for a party for rap producer Jermaine Dupri. During the course of the evening, Suge's close friend Jake Robles got into an argument that

TUPAC'S STORY

Rap star Tupac Amaru Shakur was born on June 16, 1971. He grew up in poor urban neighborhoods in New York, Baltimore, and Marin City, California. He spent his childhood surrounded by drug dealers and other criminals. He would later express this early experience through his rap lyrics.

Tupac's talent as an entertainer was apparent when he was young. When he was 13 years old, he earned a major role in a performance of the play *A Raisin in the Sun* at the world-famous Apollo Theater in Harlem. After moving to Baltimore, Tupac was accepted into the Baltimore School for the Arts, a special school where he could take classes in acting, dance, and voice. When he was 18, he was invited to join the rap group Digital Underground.

In 1992, Tupac got a part in the movie *Juice*. He received good reviews for his acting, and was soon cast in other films, such as *Poetic Justice* and *Above the Rim*. He was also getting noticed as a rapper. His second solo album, released by Interscope Records in 1993, sold more than 500,000 copies. His third album, *Me Against the World*, was even more successful.

Unfortunately, during the early 1990s Tupac was also drawing attention because of problems with the law. In one case, Tupac was found guilty of assaulting a young woman. He was sent to prison.

In 1995, Suge Knight helped to arrange for Tupac's release from prison on bail. In return, the talented young rapper agreed to record three albums for Death Row Records.

turned into a fistfight. Gunfire erupted, and Robles was fatally wounded. Police were never able to identify the shooter, but some witnesses blamed one of Puff Daddy's bodyguards.

Combs denied any knowledge of, or involvement in, the killing. He also reached out to Suge Knight in an attempt to defuse the growing East Coast–West Coast feud. Combs even sent the son of a prominent black minister to Los Angeles to try to broker a peace. But Suge refused even to speak with Puff Daddy's representative. A friend of the Death Row CEO told a reporter that Suge would "settle the beef his way. On the street."

THE SIGNING OF TUPAC

Suge Knight soon made a move that added fuel to the East Coast–West Coast fire. It involved Tupac Shakur.

In November 1994, Tupac had gone on trial in New York City for assaulting a young female fan. While the jury was deliberating, he and three friends went to a local recording studio, where Tupac was supposed to help out on a rap song being produced by an acquaintance. In the lobby of the recording studio, two armed men shot Tupac five times and took $40,000 worth of jewelry from him before fleeing.

The attackers were never caught. But Tupac didn't think their real motive had been robbery. He believed they'd been trying to kill him. And he thought he knew who had ordered the attempted hit: Sean Combs and Christopher Wallace. Wallace, also known as the Notorious B.I.G and Biggie Smalls, had been one of Tupac's closest friends. He was also the most popular rapper in Bad Boy Entertainment's lineup.

Despite his wounds, which included a gunshot to the head, Tupac was in court the day after the shooting. He heard the jury find him guilty of assault. In February 1995, the judge sentenced him to prison for 18 months to four and a half years.

Tupac's lawyers appealed the conviction. Early on, the rapper had reason to be encouraged. A court found that there were valid grounds for his appeal. Further, Tupac could be released from prison on bail as his case proceeded. Unfortunately, he had no money to post bail, which was set at $1.4 million.

Suge Knight stepped in, however. On October 12, 1995, Suge flew to New York, posted the bail money, and picked up Tupac at the prison where he had been doing his time. The two then flew directly to Los Angeles aboard Suge's private plane. Tupac signed a contract with Death Row and immediately went to work recording an album for his new label. He quickly made a contribution to Suge Knight's hip-hop hit machine. Tupac's single "California Love," produced by Dr. Dre and released on December 28, spent two weeks at #1 on the Billboard Hot 100 chart. Tupac also joined the East Coast–West Coast feud in a big way. He repeatedly dissed Puff Daddy and Bad Boy's rappers, reserving some of the nastiest insults for his former friend Biggie Smalls.

THA DOGG POUND BARKS

On October 31, while Tupac was still getting used to his new surroundings, Death Row released Tha Dogg Pound's long-awaited debut album, *Dogg Food*. It sold briskly, reaching #1 on the Billboard 200 albums chart and eventually going double-platinum.

Stylistically, *Dogg Food* broke little new ground. It was in the G-funk mold, though Daz Dillinger rather than Dr. Dre served as the main producer. (Dre was credited for mixing the album.) The usual gangs-

Tupac Shakur (left) and Suge Knight attend an awards show in 1996. The rapper signed with Death Row Records after Knight bailed him out of prison.

ta rap themes were treated, and the language was at least as *obscene* as any of Death Row's previous releases.

One track, though, seemed calculated to throw even more gas on the East Coast–West Coast fire. On "New York, New York," Daz Dillinger and Kurupt took turns boasting about their unmatched skills as MCs. The chorus featured the lines

> New York New York big city of dreams
> And everything in New York ain't always what it seems
> You might get fooled if you come from out of town
> But I'm down by law, and I'm from the Dogg Pound.

For the video, Tha Dogg Pound and guest Snoop Doggy Dogg went to New York City to film on location. Biggie Smalls objected. On a radio show, Biggie announced that the Death Row rappers were in town to diss New York. Later, as Snoop was getting ready to film a segment, a car drove up and one of its occupants sprayed the set with bullets. Fortunately, no one was injured.

ALL EYEZ ON DEATH ROW

February 1996 was a great month for Death Row Records. On the 13th, Tupac Shakur's first album for his new label, *All Eyez on Me*, was released. The two-disc, 27-track offering—which one critic summarized as 2Pac's "unabashed embrace of the gangsta lifestyle"—was a monster commercial success. *All Eyez on Me* would climb to #1 on the Billboard 200 charts and sell 5 million copies in its first two months. Eventually the RIAA would certify the album 9X platinum.

On February 20, one week after the release of *All Eyez on Me*, another of Death Row's superstars found cause for celebration. Following a trial that had lasted nearly two months, Snoop Doggy

Dogg—along with his body-guard, McKinley Lee—was acquitted of murder charges. The jury apparently accepted the claim that the August 1993 killing of Philip Waldemariam had been an act of self-defense.

> **FAST FACT**
>
> Even though it was a two-disc album, 2Pac's *All Eyez on Me* took just two weeks to record.

Suge Knight and Death Row seemed unstoppable. Interviewed in *Vibe* magazine's February 1996 issue, Tupac Shakur said, "Death Row to me is like a machine. The biggest, strongest superpower in the hip hop world."

But even superpowers can be brought down. Death Row's collapse would occur with startling speed.

5

downfall

Through the spring and summer of 1996, the animosity between the Death Row and Bad Boy camps only grew. "Five shots couldn't drop me," Tupac Shakur rapped on his single "Hit 'em Up," making it clear that Puff Daddy, Biggie Smalls, and others in their East Coast crew would pay for his attempted murder. "We're gonna kill all you," he rapped.

As the situation became more and more tense, Bad Boy Entertainment hired members of the Crips gang as bodyguards. The Crips, of course, were sworn enemies of the Bloods, and Suge Knight had long employed Mob Piru Bloods at Death Row. It seemed only a matter of time before blood was shed.

In March, while Tupac and Biggie were both backstage at the Soul

Train Music Awards in Los Angeles, a fight erupted. Bodyguards of the two rappers pulled out guns, but in the end no shots were fired and no one was seriously injured in the incident.

DEPARTURE OF DRE

Dr. Dre had grown weary of the thug atmosphere at Death Row. And it wasn't just the ongoing feud with Bad Boy Entertainment or the scuffles that often broke out at Death Row's public events, either. Inside the label's Los Angeles offices, employees were reportedly roughed up when they displeased Suge Knight. Suge appeared increasingly out of control.

In 1995, Dre served eight months in prison for violating the terms of his probation with his January 1993 DUI arrest. His time behind bars caused Dre to reevaluate his life. After getting out of

Dr. Dre left Death Row to form his own label, Aftermath Entertainment. In addition to releasing his own music, Dre signed talented unknowns to the label, such as Eminem.

prison, he married. He wanted—and thought he deserved—a happier, more peaceful existence. But, he said, "the mentality [at Death Row] is, you have to be mad at somebody in order for yourself to feel good, even to be able to make a record."

Dre also wanted to expand his musical horizons. He thought that gangsta rap had reached a creative dead end. He believed that Death Row should branch out into other genres, such as reggae and jazz. But, with the profits from gangsta rap records pouring in, nobody at the label agreed.

In June 1996, Dre left Death Row, the label he had cofounded. He started a new label, Aftermath Entertainment.

The loss of its most visionary producer was certainly a blow to Death Row. In Dre's absence, Daz Dillinger was tapped to supervise the production of Snoop Doggy Dogg's upcoming second album, scheduled for release in the fall of 1996. Tupac Shakur also went to work on a new album. Tupac relied on relatively inexperienced producers.

DEATH IN LAS VEGAS

On the night of September 7, 1996, Tupac, Suge Knight, and members of the Death Row entourage were at the MGM Grand Hotel in Las Vegas to watch a heavyweight boxing match. After the bout had ended and they were leaving, Tupac spotted a young man named Orlando Anderson. Anderson was a member of the Crips gang. He also, it is believed, had taken part in the August 1996 beating of one of Tupac's bodyguards, who was a member of the Bloods. During that assault, the bodyguard's Death Row medallion had been ripped from his neck.

In 1996, Death Row Records owned a nightclub in Las Vegas called Club 662. When asked what the name meant, Suge Knight explained that the number 662 spells out M-O-B on a telephone keypad. But he refused to say whether that was a reference to the Mob Piru Bloods.

At the MGM Grand, Tupac walked up to Anderson and threw a punch. Immediately, his bodyguards joined in. They pummeled and kicked the young man. So did Suge Knight. The beating lasted no more than half a minute, and the Death Row entourage hustled out of the MGM Grand before police arrived. But the incident was captured on the hotel's security cameras.

A couple hours later, a caravan of vehicles carrying the Death Row crew was cruising down the Las Vegas Strip. They were headed to Club 662, a nightclub owned by Death Row Records. Suge Knight was driving the lead car, a BMW, with Tupac riding in the passenger seat.

The windows were down, and many people along the crowded Strip recognized the popular rapper. Around 11:15 P.M., the BMW stopped at a busy intersection. Tupac was chatting with a group of female fans when a white Cadillac pulled up alongside the passenger side of the BMW. Someone in the Cadillac poked a pistol out the window and began firing. Tupac was hit four times. Three of his wounds were in the chest. Suge escaped with a graze to the head.

Tupac was taken to the University Medical Center in Las Vegas. He died there on September 13. He was 25 years old.

To this day, the murder of Tupac Shakur remains unsolved. But there is no shortage of speculation about who killed him, or who

The bullet-riddled vehicle in which Tupac Shakur was fatally wounded on September 7, 1996. In the background, Las Vegas police are interviewing Suge Knight, who had been driving the car when the shooting occurred.

ordered him killed. Rumors about who was behind Tupac's death began to fly almost immediately after the shooting.

Some people considered Orlando Anderson the most likely killer. He had a motive—revenge for the beating Tupac and his bodyguards had inflicted only hours before—as well as a long criminal record. Las Vegas police questioned Anderson but never charged him. He was killed in a gang-related shoot-out in 1998.

With all the bad blood between Bad Boy Entertainment and Death Row, many people theorized that Tupac was a victim of the East Coast–West Coast hip-hop feud. Some of these theories found their way into print. The *Los Angeles Times*, for example, published a story claiming Biggie Smalls had ordered the hit on his former friend. But much of the information upon which the story was based turned out to be untrue.

Biggie himself was murdered in a manner that was very similar to the way in which Tupac had been killed. Biggie had gone to Los Angeles to film a video and appear at an awards show. Around 1 A.M. on March 9, 1997, he was sitting in the passenger seat of an SUV that had stopped at a red light. A car pulled up alongside. Its driver pointed a pistol at Biggie and began firing. The rapper was hit four times in the chest.

> **FAST FACT**
>
> Between 1996, when Tupac Shakur was killed, and 2010, at least nine people associated with Death Row were murdered. They included four of Suge Knight's closest friends.

As with the killing of Tupac Shakur, the murder of Biggie Smalls remains unsolved. But many people immediately concluded that the motive in Biggie's slaying was revenge for the killing of Tupac. And, though he was never

Even after his death, Tupac Shakur remained one of hip-hop's most popular and iconic artists. Here he is pictured at the MTV Video Awards three days before being shot in Las Vegas.

charged, many suspected Suge Knight of ordering the hit.

Interestingly, a former Los Angeles Police Department detective claimed that Suge had masterminded the killings of Biggie *and* Tupac. The former detective, Russell Poole, suggested that Tupac had been planning to leave Death Row, and Suge ordered his murder to prevent that from happening. Poole explained the lack of evidence to support his theory by claiming that police had engaged in a cover-up.

END OF AN ERA

On November 5, 1996, about seven weeks after Tupac Shakur died, Death Row released his album *The Don Killuminati: The 7 Day Theory*. Tupac had adopted the stage name Makaveli for the project. A week later, the label released *Tha Doggfather*, from Snoop Doggy Dogg.

Both albums were big commercial successes. *The Don Killuminati: The 7 Day Theory* debuted at #1 on the Billboard 200 albums chart. It went on to sell more than 4 million copies. *Tha Doggfather* also debuted at #1 and would be certified 2X platinum. Death Row didn't appear to have lost its knack for churning out hits. But the label was about to be sent into a tailspin from which it would never recover.

In early 1997, Suge Knight's run-ins with the law finally caught up to him. Two years before, he'd pled guilty to assault in the 1992 beating of the Stanley brothers. He'd received probation in that case. But Suge's participation in the beating of Orlando Anderson at the MGM Grand Hotel in Las Vegas violated the terms of his probation. A judge sentenced him to nine years in prison.

Suge tried to run Death Row Records from behind bars. But he was unable to hold the label together.

Death Row did release three albums in 1997. One of them, the soundtrack *Gang Related*, went double-platinum. But sales for the other two were disappointing.

Suge Knight was sent to prison in 1997. Without him, Death Row Records soon fell apart, as the label's most popular artists broke away.

The soundtrack *Gridlock'd* was certified gold (500,000 copies) but became the first Death Row album that failed to go platinum. *Necessary Roughness,* the solo album of The Lady of Rage, didn't even reach gold status.

In January 1998, Interscope dropped its distribution agreement with Death Row. Soon after, the label's top artists began leaving. Claiming that he feared for his life, Snoop Doggy Dogg was the first and biggest star to go. His departure touched off a bitter war of words with Suge. Nate Dogg and Kurupt were next to leave. Daz Dillinger—whom Suge had appointed his second-in-command—left shortly after the release of his debut solo album, *Retaliation, Revenge and Get Back.* With Death Row in disarray, the album had received almost no promotion, and sales were disappointing.

Although Death Row signed new artists to replace the stars it lost, the label failed to release a single album by any of these newcomers. Instead, Death Row put out several **compilation** albums and even an album of previously unreleased tracks from Snoop Doggy Dogg. All but one of these albums flopped. The exception was *2Pac—Greatest Hits.* Released in November 1998, the two-disc, 25-track collection of Tupac Shakur songs would be certified 9X platinum.

Suge Knight got out of prison on **parole** in 2001, after serving four years of his nine-year sentence. He renamed his record label Tha Row and signed Lisa "Left Eye" Lopes, who had gained fame with the R&B group TLC. But Lopes was killed in a car accident in April 2002, before she could complete an album. In December of that year, Suge Knight punched a parking lot attendant. That violated the terms of his parole. In 2003, he received a 10-month prison sentence. He got out in 2004.

Lisa "Left Eye" Lopes made news when she signed with Tha Row
Records. However, she died in a car crash before completing an
album for Suge Knight's label.

In April 2006, Suge Knight and his label filed for bankruptcy after two former associates, Lydia and Michael Harris, won a $107 million settlement from them. In June 2008, the assets of Death Row Records were finally sold at auction for $24 million. The buyer was the New York–based Global Music Group Inc.

SOUND OF THE TIME

Death Row Records had lasted only 17 years, from its founding to its liquidation at auction. And the label had only really flourished for

Suge Knight is interviewed by reporters as he leaves the Los Angeles County Jail. The founder of Death Row Records has had many encounters with the law since the label fell apart.

about five years, from the release of *The Chronic* in 1992 to Suge Knight's incarceration in 1997.

But during that brief time, Death Row produced a string of important albums. These albums didn't simply shape the gangsta rap genre. They also sold millions of copies, taking gangsta rap from a small, mainly African-American audience into the mainstream. While the lyrics spoke to the violence, disorder, and despair of life in black ghettos, the music was also embraced by white adolescents and youth. For many of them, gangsta rap was simply great party music. Death Row had, in the words of writer Erik Boehlert, "managed to do what so few other record companies have done over the decades: perfectly capture, or even define, the sound of its time."

Chronology

1991 Death Row Records is founded by Suge Knight and Dr. Dre.

1992 Death Row signs a distribution agreement with Interscope and releases Dre's first solo album, *The Chronic*. It becomes a big hit.

1993 In August, Snoop Doggy Dogg is involved in the fatal shooting of a Los Angeles gang member.

In November, Death Row releases *Doggystyle*, Snoop's debut solo album. It becomes the first rap album to debut at #1 on the Billboard 200 charts.

1994 In March, Death Row releases the motion picture soundtrack *Above the Rim*.

Another soundtrack, *Murder Was the Case*, is released in October. It reaches #1 on the Billboard 200 charts.

1995 In February, Tupac Shakur is sentenced to prison for up to four and a half years for assaulting a young female fan.

At the Source Hip-Hop Awards in August, Suge Knight publicly disses Sean "Puff Daddy" Combs, head of the rival Bad Boy Entertainment label. Many observers believe this marked the beginning of the East Coast–West Coast hip-hop feud.

In September, following a nationwide ad campaign against gangsta rap led by C. Delores Tucker and William Bennett, the media giant Time Warner announces that it will sell its share of Interscope.

In October, Suge Knight bails Tupac Shakur out of prison, and Tupac signs with Death Row.

Chronology

Dogg Food, the debut album of Tha Dogg Pound, is released October 31. It reaches #1 on the Billboard 200 charts.

1996 Tupac's *All Eyez on Me* is released on February 13. It will sell 5 million copies within two months.

Snoop Doggy Dogg is found not guilty of murder on February 20.

Dr. Dre leaves Death Row Records in June and forms his own label, Aftermath Entertainment.

On September 7, Tupac Shakur is gunned down in Las Vegas. He dies on September 13.

In November, Death Row releases *The Don Killuminati: The 7 Day Theory* and *Tha Doggfather.* Both reach #1 on the Billboard 200 charts.

1997 Suge Knight is sentenced to nine years in prison for violating his probation in an earlier assault case.

On March 9, Biggie Smalls is murdered in Los Angeles.

1998 Snoop Doggy Dogg, Nate Dogg, Kurupt, and Daz Dillinger all leave Death Row.

2001 Suge Knight is released from prison on parole.

2003 Suge Knight serves a 10-month prison sentence after assaulting a parking lot attendant in late 2002.

2006 Suge Knight and Death Row file for bankruptcy.

2008 In June, Death Row is sold to Global Music Group, an independent label based in New York, for $24 million.

2012 In February, Suge Knight is arrested in Las Vegas for drug possession.

GLOSSARY

associate's degree—an academic degree usually awarded after two years of study by a community college or junior college.

battery—a criminal offense involving harmful, offensive, or unwanted contact with another person.

boycott—to refuse to have any dealings with a business or other organization, usually as a means of forcing changes in policy.

compilation—a musical collection that is made up of previously released material and that often incorporates the work of multiple artists.

crossover—the process by which an artist or group popular only with fans of a particular type of music becomes popular with fans of other types of music; an artistic work that achieves popularity outside its original genre.

debut—the first appearance by a performer; to make one's first appearance.

entourage—a group of associates who travel with a high-ranking or important person.

explicit—fully expressed; leaving nothing to the imagination.

genre—a category of artistic work.

glamorize—to make something seem more interesting, exciting, or desirable that it really is; to glorify.

mogul—a person who has great power or influence in a particular field.

no contest—in the law, a plea by which a person charged with a crime doesn't dispute the charge but doesn't admit guilt.

obscene—disgusting; morally repulsive.

parole—the release of a prisoner before all of his or her sentence has been served.

probation—the suspension of a prison sentence for someone convicted of a crime, allowing the person to remain free as long as he or she stays out of further legal trouble and cooperates with terms of supervision.

royalties—payments due to a writer or composer based on the number of copies sold.

sampling—a musical production technique, used especially in hip-hop, in which parts of other artists' recordings are incorporated into a new song.

tour de force—an extraordinary display of skill.

Further Reading

Bradley, Adam. *Book of Rhymes: The Poetics of Hip Hop.* New York: Basic Civitas Books, 2009.

Bynoe, Yvonne. *Encyclopedia of Rap and Hip-Hop Culture.* Westport, CT: Greenwood, 2006.

Carlson-Berne, Emma. *Snoop Dogg.* Broomall, PA: Mason Crest Publishers, 2006.

Scott, Cathy. *The Killing of Tupac Shakur.* Las Vegas: Huntington Press, 2002.

Sullivan, Randall. *LAbyrinth: A Detective Investigates the Murders of Tupac Shakur and Notorious B.I.G.* New York: Atlantic Monthly Press, 2002.

Internet Resources

http://rap.about.com/od/hiphop101/a/hiphoptimeline.htm

This site provides a detailed timeline of hip-hop.

http://www.dr-dre.com/

Fans can find a wealth of information about Dr. Dre, who cofounded Death Row Records and pioneered G-funk, at this site.

http://www.snoopdogg.com/home.aspx

The official site of Snoop Dogg.

http://www.deathrowmusic.com

The official Web site of the reorganized Death Row Records lists upcoming releases and news about the company.

http://foia.fbi.gov/foiaindex/cripsbloods.htm

An extensive archive of newspaper and magazine stories on the Crips and Bloods, as well as a research study on the gangs written by the University of the Pacific McGeorge School of Law, can be downloaded from this Web site maintained by the Federal Bureau of Investigation.

index

Entries in ***bold italic*** refer to captions

TREY WHITE is a freelance writer whose interests include politics, sports, and music. His favorite rapper is Jay-Z.